Non-Fiction
Teaching Notes

Andrew Hammond

OXFORD
UNIVERSITY PRESS

Contents

Introduction

TreeTops Non-fiction is an exciting extension to the *TreeTops* range. All the titles have been chosen to appeal to 7–11 year olds and have an appropriate reading ability level at their particular Stage. *TreeTops* Stages follow on from the *Oxford Reading Tree* Stages, and are designed to be used flexibly with your individual pupil's reading ability. The levelling guide on page 5 gives you an indication of how the Stages correspond to the Year and age of the average pupil, together with the relevant match from the National Curriculum Level or Scottish, Northern Irish and Welsh equivalents.

Each book includes a Contents page, an Index and/or a Glossary of specialist terms or equivalent. These features enable teachers to develop children's information retrieval skills. In addition features of non-fiction texts, such as sub-headings, text boxes, and captions help children learn to skim read a text for information. The series aims to fascinate children with surprising and interesting information.

How to introduce the books

Before reading the book, always read the title and talk about the possible content. Encourage the children to articulate what they already know about the subject, what they would like to find out and how they will use this book to do it. Complete the reading session with the pupils telling you what they have learned.

This booklet provides suggestions for using the book with groups of pupils or individuals. Suggestions are also provided for speaking and listening, further reading activities, ICT links and writing. These may be used as a follow on to the reading or used at another time.

Guided Reading Cards with built-in comprehension are available for each book. These provide detailed guidance for using the book for guided reading. Parental notes are included with each individual book.

Cross-curricular links with QCA/NLS objectives

Title	QCA Cross-curricular links	NLS objectives
Explosions	Science 6D Reversible and irreversible changes	Y6 T3 T15 to secure understanding of the features of explanatory texts Y6 T3 T19 to review a range of non-fiction text types and their characteristics, discussing when a writer might choose to write in a given style
Pests, Plagues and Parasites	Science 6B Micro-organisms 6A Interdependence and adaptation	Y6 T2 T17 to read and understand examples of official language and its characteristic features, e.g. discussing consumer information Y6 T3 T15 to secure understanding of the features of explanatory texts
Our Earth is Unique	Science 6A Interdependence and adaptation Geography 18 Connecting ourselves to the world	Y6 T2 T15 to recognise how arguments are constructed to be effective through, e.g. appealing to the known views and feelings of the audience Y6 T2 T18 to construct effective arguments: supporting and illustrating points persuasively
Arms and Armour	History 18 What was it like to live here in the past?	Y6 T3 T15 to secure understanding of the features of explanatory texts Y6 T3 T18 to secure the skills of skimming, scanning and efficient reading so that research is fast and effective Y6 T2 T10 to use different genres as models to write, e.g. short extracts
Let's Go to the Planets!	Science 5E Earth, Sun and Moon 5C Gases around us 6E Forces in action	Y6 T2 T16 to identify the features of balanced written arguments which summarise different sides of an argument Y6 T3 18 to secure the skills of skimming, scanning and efficient reading so that research is fast and effective
Planet Granite	Science 3C Characteristics of materials 3D Rocks and Soils	Y6 T2 T19 to write a balanced report of a controversial issue Y6 T3 T19 to review a range of non-fiction text types and their characteristics, discussing when a writer might choose to write in a given style

Levels Chart

Title	TreeTops Stage 16	England NC level	Scotland	Northern Ireland	Wales
Explosions	Year 6 Term 3 Ages 10–11	Level 4/5	Level D/E	*Reading Activities:* b, f, g, i Outcomes: e, f, g, i, k *Writing* Opportunities: b, c Outcomes: b, c, d	*Reading:* Range: 1, 3, 4, 5 Skills: 5, 6, 7, 8 Language development: 1, 2 *Writing:* Range: 1, 4, 5 Skills: 2, 3, 8 Language development: 1, 2, 4, 6
Parasites, Pests and Plagues	Year 6 Terms 2 and 3 Ages 10–11	Level 4/5	Level D/E		
Our Earth is Unique	Year 6 Term 2 Ages 10–11	Level 4/5	Level D/E		
Arms and Armour	Year 6 Terms 2 and 3 Ages 10–11	Level 4/5	Level D/E		
Let's Go to the Planets!	Year 6 Terms 2 and 3 Ages 10–11	Level 4/5	Level D/E		
Planet Granite	Year 6 Terms 2 and 3 Ages 10–11	Level 4/5	Level D/E		

Explosions

Reading the book with individuals or guided reading groups

Introducing the book

- Look together at the front cover and discuss the title. Invite the children to suggest the type of texts that might feature in this book.
- Explain to the children that there are many non-fiction text types featured in the book, including information texts, explanatory texts, instructional texts, chronological reports and discussion texts.
- Look together at the Contents page and invite the children to analyse the type of text each heading might suggest.

Strategy check

- Remind the children of the purpose of a glossary. Turn to page 31 and read through the Glossary together. Remind them that they may refer to it when a word appears in bold print.
- When the children encounter difficult words that are not in bold print, they may: read around the word to glean meaning and sense from the surrounding sentences; look closely at the word to identify possible clues in prefixes/suffixes; use a dictionary.

Focus of reading

- Explain to the children that you want them to find as much information as they can about fireworks from within the book – including how they work, the effects they can create, the dangers involved and the times when they are used throughout the year.

- Equipped with this knowledge, they will be writing their own mini-projects on fireworks that will feature a range of very different text types.

Independent reading

- As the children read, encourage them to begin compiling notes in their rough books/on PCs, scanning texts for relevant information that may be extracted and referred to later.
- Encourage children to think about the different language features of each text within the book – and to identify common techniques and devices in use, so that they may model the texts in their writing projects.

Return and respond to the text

- Invite the children to share some of the knowledge they have learned about fireworks.
- Compile a 'firework calendar' on the board onto which all the year's events at which fireworks are lit could be recorded. The children may share information from the book and from their own knowledge and experience.

Further reading activities

- Set the children the task of finding out exactly how volcanoes are formed and the devastating effects an eruption can cause.
- Ask them to reproduce this information in their own explanatory texts using annotated diagrams, captions and headed paragraphs.
- Remind the children of the language features of explanatory texts, modelled on pages 20–21, for example, and including: technical words and phrases; connectives to show sequence; words and devices to show cause and effect.

Speaking and listening activities

- Revisit pages 14–15 together. Hold a discussion on whether or not fireworks should be restricted to professional displays only. You may wish to formally debate the following motion: 'This House believes that firework licences should be introduced, making it illegal for firework displays to be held other than by licensed professionals.'

- Ask the children to work in pairs to produce a short two-minute presentation on how to make popcorn. They may act out the scene as though it were part of a daytime television cookery programme!

ICT links

- Ask the children to produce a persuasive poster warning viewers of the dangers of fireworks and the importance of handling them with care at all times. They may use a range of IT techniques and devices to create their posters – and then include them in the writing project below.

Writing

- Explain that the task for the children is to produce their own mini-project on fireworks. It will be feature a range of model text types, including an explanatory text, an information text, an instructional text, a discussion text and a persuasive poster.

Pests, Plagues and Parasites

Reading the book with individuals or guided reading groups

Introducing the book

- Consider the front cover together. *What sort of book might this be, based on the title? Why has the author used alliteration here? Is it effective?*
- Ask the children to make a note of the sort of information they expect to find in this book, e.g. types, locations, habits and effects of parasites.
- Elicit the children's prior knowledge of plagues. What famous plagues will they expect to find in this book? Do they know how plagues can spread?
- Turn to the Contents page and consider together whether each chapter will involve parasites, pests or plagues.
- Discuss with the children the type of audience, purpose, layout and language features of informative and explanatory texts. Flick through the book together and highlight the use of headings, diagrams, annotations and captions.

Strategy check

- Revisit the purpose and layout of a glossary. Turn to page 30 and observe how the Glossary is arranged alphabetically.
- Explain that these words feature in the book they are about to read, and are usually highlighted in bold print to aid identification and understanding.
- Discuss the strategies the children can employ when unfamiliar words are encountered in context.

Focus of reading

- As the children read they should pay particular attention to the information on head lice, in preparation for writing a leaflet. Encourage them to consider the way information is presented in the book – through informative, explanatory and instructional text.
- Highlight the author's frequent use of instruction text in the 'Beat the bug' boxes. Discuss the language features of instruction text, such as: imperatives; bullet points; short, factual phrases or sentences.

Independent reading

- As the children read the text, check that they are referring to the Glossary for meanings when needed.
- Encourage the children to use both the Index and Contents page when looking for particular information.

Return and respond to the text

- Guide the children's feedback on head lice by recording key questions on the board, e.g. 'What are they?' 'Why do they live on us?' 'How are they spread?' What can we do when we have them?'
- Encourage the children to locate and discuss good examples of text types they have found in the book – and to discuss together how they see their information leaflets shaping up.
- Share pages within the book that the children think have been well designed and identify the features that work well.

Further reading activities

- Ask the children to look through the book to retrieve information on the types of pests that may be living in our homes and where they can be found.
- Ask the children to note this information on a diagram of the interior of a house, using labels to show the types and locations of the pests.

Speaking and listening activities

- Revisit pages 16–17 together and read through the story of 'Balder the Beautiful'. Ask the children to divide into small groups. Each group enact this story through role play, separating the story into scenes, perhaps with a narrator.

- Ask the children to work in pairs to produce a short presentation on The Black Death, explaining where it originated from, how it spread across the world and its devastating effects.

ICT links

- Ask the children to use their IT skills to produce the information leaflet on head lice, as described in the writing activity. They will need to consider visual impact as well as content.
- Invite the children to research head lice using various multimedia sources including the Internet, CD ROMS, library books and magazines.

Writing

- Ask the pupils to produce a concise and informative leaflet for children, exposing the myth of head lice.
- The leaflet must contain at least one information text, one explanation and one short set of instructions. The children may choose to include annotated diagrams and artwork too.
- Encourage the children to consider the audience, purpose and language features of the texts they are writing. They will need to make their leaflets clear, concise and eye-catching.

Our Earth is Unique

Reading the book with individuals or guided reading groups

Introducing the book

- Consider the front cover and discuss the title. What sort of book do the children expect to find?
- Introduce the idea of uniqueness. What do the children think the title is suggesting about our planet and the way we regard it? *Will there be a message for us in this book? A moral at the end?*
- Revise some of the typical features of non-fiction texts, including contents, index, glossary, sub-headings, captions and annotated diagrams.

Strategy check

- Remind the children of the strategies they have been employing when encountering new and unfamiliar words. Remind them of the purpose and layout of a glossary.
- Draw the pupils' attention to the key words in bold print and explain that these will be included in the Glossary on page 32. Model this process by focusing on the word 'adaptation' on page 8 and looking it up together in the Glossary.

Focus of reading

- Ask the children to think of the title more as a question: How is our Earth unique? Encourage them to consider how and why life has been able to thrive *here* rather than on other planets.
- Throughout their reading, encourage the children to consider the author's intentions beyond giving us

information, i.e. not only to increase our knowledge of the world, but also to educate and instruct the way we think about the Earth.

Independent reading

- Check that the children are reading and understanding the text: ask questions; pause to discuss points raised; observe reading strategies.
- Encourage the children to take cues not only from the text itself but also from illustrations, diagrams and captions.
- Remind the children of the importance of headings and sub-headings in sorting the knowledge they retrieve from the book.

Return and respond to the text

- Begin by eliciting the children's prior knowledge of the types of places found on Earth. Can they identify the main types?
- Set the children the task of ascertaining how many different types of place (or 'biomes') there are on this planet and to be able to talk about each type in detail.
- As they read, ask the children to begin compiling sample questions that they may give to other readers to assess their reading comprehension.

Further reading activities

- Ask the children to consider how, and when, life began on Earth. As they read the text, invite the children to begin compiling a timeline for life on Earth, beginning with simple life forms (bacteria) to more complex organisms.
- Encourage the children to see how we as humans are comparatively new arrivals on the planet – guests of those species who have lived here for many years longer. Introduce the idea that we have a responsibility to preserve the planet for future generations and species.

Speaking and listening activities

- Ask the children to plan, rehearse and perform a short 'television broadcast' designed to prompt viewers to take more care of our planet.
- Consider some key messages: the Earth is unique and precious but we, as humans, have the potential to save or destroy the species that surround us.
- The short broadcast will need to be concise, punchy and very persuasive to make viewers stop and think!

ICT links

- Encourage the children to research further information on a key environmental issue (e.g. global warming). Good websites include:
  www.woodland-trust.org.uk/discovery
  www.oxfam.org.uk/coolplanet
  www.uk.oneworld.net/penguin/biodiversity/home

Writing

- Ask the children to use the information they have retrieved from this book to produce a poster that celebrates the Earth's uniqueness and encourages viewers to take a more active role in preserving the planet.
- The children will need to revisit the text and make notes, extracting key information that will help to create an informative but persuasive poster.
- Encourage the children to find amazing facts about the Earth – evidence that will make us, as humans, feel lucky to be here!

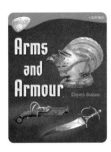

Arms and Armour

Reading the book with individuals or guided reading groups

Introducing the book

- Consider the front page together – its title and artwork. Invite suggestions from the children on the type of texts they can expect: non-chronological reports; recounts; explanations.
- Look together at the Contents page. Read the titles and invite the children to say which ones sound particularly appealing and why.
- Read pages 4 and 5. Ask the children to say what type of text is featured on these pages. *Is there a paragraph that stands out particularly from the rest?* (The introductory paragraph is written as a piece of prose – perhaps from a story or fictional diary.) *Why has this been included?* (To set the scene and to place the weapons in a real context.)

Strategy check

- Remind the children about the purpose and layout of a glossary. Highlight words printed in bold print in the book, which can be found in the Glossary on page 31.
- Explain also that the pupils will encounter other words in this text that may be unfamiliar, namely the weapons and their origins. The meanings for these will lie within the explanations and reports, so they will need to read the text carefully as they go along, not least so that they can answer the quiz on page 30.

Focus of reading

- Ask the children to focus particularly on where the weapons featured in the book originate from. This information will be useful in a subsequent writing activity.
- Invite the children, as they move through the book, to consider how weaponry has progressed in design and sophistication through the ages and to identify which weapons and battle procedures remain largely unchanged today.

Independent reading

- Check that the pupils are reading and understanding the text carefully, using the Glossary where appropriate and eliciting meaning from explanations and reports.
- Pause and reflect on the effectiveness of the prose style introductory paragraphs, sharing children's responses and encouraging the children to imagine the weapons and armour actually in use.

Return and respond to the text

- Ask the children to explain which weapons they prefer and why. *Which would have had the greatest impact on the enemy?*
- Collate on the board a record of where the different arms and armour originate from around the world.
- Turn together to pages 12 and 13. Read the introductory paragraph and the subsequent information texts on longbows and crossbows. Can the children identify what makes the first paragraph stand out? *What are the language techniques and devices used here that do not appear elsewhere on these pages?* (powerful imagery through adjectives, abstract nouns and metaphor)

Further reading activities

● Invite the children to use the information in the book to consider, and perhaps write a report on, how wars were once fought. They will need to sift through the text, retrieving information on weapon capabilities, and defence systems.

Speaking and listening activities

● Invite the children to work through the quiz on page 30, in pairs or small groups. As they find answers, they will need to make a note of them so that they can feed back to the class in a final plenary.

● Hold a class quiz, in which teams take turns facing a question from the quizmaster. They may/may not refer to the book.

● Hold a class discussion/debate on the best ways of resolving conflict. Is violence the only solution?

ICT links

● Encourage the children to use IT skills when completing the writing tasks.

● Research further information on arms and armour using the Internet, books, CD ROMS and magazines.

Writing

● Ask the children to construct a visual information text to show where the different weapons and defence systems originate from around the world. Global maps may be retrieved from the Internet, or from other sources.

● Ask the children to write a chronological report, to show how arms and armour evolved through the ages.

● Invite the children to write their own descriptive prose, depicting some of the weapons in use on a battle field.

Let's Go to the Planets!
Reading the book with individuals or guided reading groups

Introducing the book

- Look together at the book's front cover and title. Ask the children to suggest what type of text this might be. Consider how appealing the title is.
- Read the Contents page together and discuss the various chapter headings listed. Invite the pupils to suggest what each one might be about.
- Consider together the purpose and layout of the Glossary and Index texts at the back of the book. Which phrases are already familiar to the children and which are new?
- Turn together to pages 4–5. Highlight the differences between the narrative paragraphs and the rest of the page: the use of the present continuous tense; descriptive language to set the scene; the use of questions and exclamations to engage the reader.
- Contrast these features with the more formal characteristics of informative and explanatory texts.

Strategy check

- Remind the children of the importance of actively using the Glossary to look up new words and using the Index for guiding and focusing their reading and research.
- Emphasise, too, the usefulness of artwork and photographs throughout the book, in aiding understanding and engaging readers' interest.

Focus of reading

- Ask the children to focus particularly on the way in which space travel has evolved over the years. The children may use notebooks to record significant milestones in the space race.
- Ask the children to focus on the way in which our solar system is made up – names/locations of planets and any interesting facts about each one.

Independent reading

- As they read, check that the children are using visual and written cues in order to retrieve and retain key information about the planets in the book.
- In a text that presents a lot of information on each double-page spread, the children need to remember to read each page from top left to bottom right as a general rule, pausing to view visuals and read the annotations that accompany them.

Return and respond to the text

- Invite the children to form pairs or small groups and to share their findings on the planets in our solar system. Can they find ways of remembering them all? (mnemonics, rhymes, etc.)
- Ask the children to think about the type of text they may be reading, thinking at all times about the purpose, layout and language features of each text type.

Further reading activities

- Ask the children to consider the impact of the lunar landing in 1969. Re-read pages 10–11 and try to imagine how people must have felt when they saw the first pictures of the astronauts' arrival on the Moon.
- Invite the children to sift through the text, eliciting the salient points of this news story and to present them in a journalistic style text, taken from an imaginary newspaper article published at the time.

Speaking and listening activities

- Revisit pages 12–13. Hold a class debate, in which the following motion is debated: 'This House believes that one should address the problems on this Earth before investing billions of dollars on seeking out new worlds'.
- In pairs, or small groups, invite the children to consider the questions on page 30, using them to guide their interaction and discourse. Each group may present their findings to the rest of the class in a plenary.

ICT links

- Invite the children to find out more about the planets by using the Internet, books, CD ROMS and magazines.
- Encourage the children to make use of IT resources to complete the writing task(s).

Writing

- Ask the children to write a balanced discussion text, presenting the opposing views on space exploration. They may add an editorial section at the end in which they offer their own response to the issue.

- Ask the children to construct their own 'Top Trump' style cards for the planets in our solar system. Suggestions for the 'categories' are: size, distance from Sun, number of moons, temperature on surface. Pages 6–7 will be useful here.

- Invite the children to construct their own timeline (visual chronological report) on which they plot the landmark expeditions and research missions to date.

Planet Granite

Reading the book with individuals or guided reading groups

Introducing the book

- Look together at the front cover and discuss the title. What sort of book are the children expecting to find? A science fiction story? An encyclopedia on space? Or perhaps a book of poetry?
- Look at the Contents page together and revisit the children's expectations.
- Remind the children of the function of contents, index and glossary pages.
- Discuss the purpose, layout and common features of non-chronological reports.
- Turn together to pages 4–5. Discuss the style of writing – written in the first person, with a strong narrative, like a tour guide through the book. What do the children think? Ask: *Is this an effective way of presenting complicated information?*

Strategy check

- Remind the children that, like other books in the series, this will contain certain words in bold print, and that these may be found in the Glossary (page 31) with definitions and explanations alongside.
- The children will need to read the texts carefully and learn to extract meaning from explanatory paragraphs – like taking stone from a quarry! You may wish for them to make summary notes as they proceed.

Focus of reading

- Essentially the focus for the children's reading is to ascertain the types of stones we use around the world and the pros and cons of each.
- As they move through the book, encourage the children to identify how granite, and other stones like it, becomes a polished granite floor from being a rock in the ground! *How is it excavated? How is it shaped, cut and delivered?*

Independent reading

- Invite the children to piece together a 'working day in the life' of Richard. *What does his job involve?* Would the children like to work with stone in this way?
- *What would be your favourite stone and why?*

Return and respond to the text

- Share feedback from the children on the types of stones and their characteristics. Record these on the board.
- Invite the children to suggest ways in which stone could be sorted and classified. *If you found a stone in a field and wanted to identify it, what questions might you ask?* Could the children design their own binary sorting tree, which could be used to sort and classify unknown stones?
- Discuss the children's favourite stones. *Why do we regard some as more precious than others?*

Further reading activities

- Put Post-it notes over the answers to the quiz on page 30. Ask them to work through the questions, writing answers in their books, or discussing them orally in pairs.
- Ask the children to set some of their own comprehension questions for each other, on the types of stones in the book and the methods of extraction mentioned.

Speaking and listening activities

- Turn together to pages 18–19 and read the text again. Discuss the terms 'non-renewable' and 'regenerate' to ensure understanding.
- Initiate a discussion, or class debate, on the question of whether or not we should be extracting stone in such large quantities around the world. You may wish to use the following motion: 'This House believes that as a non-renewable source, major limits should be placed on the excavation of stone'.

ICT links

- The children may use IT to assist in the writing tasks below.

- Encourage the children to conduct further research on stones. Useful websites include:
www.ancientroute.com/resource/stone and
www.britarch.ac.uk/educate

Writing

- Ask the children to produce their own discussion text, featuring the opposing views on the excavation and sale of stone around the world and including a short editorial conclusion in which they express their own response.

- Invite the pupils to create their own chronological explanation in which the 'journey' of a stone is tracked from the moment of extraction to the sale and installation of a kitchen work top or fireplace. They may use artwork, captions, labels and headings to accompany their writing.

Links to other TreeTops and OUP titles

Oxford Literacy Web Non-fiction KS2
TreeTops True Stories Stages 15–16
Oxford Connections

TreeTops Non-fiction Stage 16	*TreeTops* and OUP titles with similar subjects/themes
Explosions	*TreeTops* Non-fiction *Under the Volcano*
Parasites, Pests and Plagues	*TreeTops* True Stories *Black Death*
Our Earth is Unique	*TreeTops* Non-fiction *The Power of Nature* *TreeTops* Non-fiction *Animals and Us* Oxford Connections *Interdependence and Adaptation* Oxford Connections *Mountains* Oxford Connections *Water and Rivers*
Arms and Armour	Oxford Connections *The Greeks* Oxford Connections *Roman Britain*
Let's Go to the Planets!	*TreeTops* Non-fiction *The Moon* Web Weavers *Earth in Space* *TreeTops* True Stories *Race Against Time*
Planet Granite	

OXFORD
UNIVERSITY PRESS

Great Clarendon Street, Oxford OX2 6DP

Oxford University Press is a department of the University of Oxford. It furthers the University's objective of excellence in research, scholarship, and education by publishing worldwide in

Oxford New York
Auckland Cape Town Dar es Salaam Hong Kong Karachi Kuala Lumpur Madrid Melbourne Mexico City Nairobi New Delhi Shanghai Taipei Toronto

With offices in
Argentina Austria Brazil Chile Czech Republic France Greece Guatemala Hungary Italy Japan Poland Portugal Singapore South Korea Switzerland Thailand Turkey Ukraine Vietnam Oxford is a registered trade mark of Oxford University Press in the UK and in certain other countries

British Library Cataloguing in Publication Data

Data available

ISBN 978-0-19-917951-0

10 9 8 7 6 5

Page make-up by Fakenham Photosetting Ltd, Fakenham, Norfolk

Printed in China by Imago